C000254671

STAFFORDSHIRE MOORLANDS
AND THE CHURNET VALLEY

• PHOTOGRAPHS OF DAYS GONE BY •

Page one: At the bottom of Thorncliffe Bank

This page: Cheddleton Flint Mill. One of the two waterwheels turning in an icy spell

Page three: "Gone Fishin' " on the Leek arm of the Caldon Canal forty years ago

STAFFORDSHIRE MOORLANDS
AND THE CHURNET VALLEY

• PHOTOGRAPHS OF DAYS GONE BY •

Lindsey Porter & Cathryn Walton

Published by

Landmark Publishing Ltd,

Waterloo House, 12 Compton, Ashbourne, Derbyshire DE6 1DA England
Tel: (01335) 347349 Fax: (01335) 347303
e-mail: landmark@clara.net www.landmarkpublishing.co.uk

1st edition

ISBN 1 901 522 85 7

© Lindsey Porter and Cathryn Walton 2000

The rights of Lindsey Porter and Cathryn Walton as authors of this work
has been asserted by them in accordance with the Copyright,
Design and Patents Act, 1993.

All rights reserved. No part of this publication may be reproduced, stored in a
retrieval system or transmitted in any form or by any means, electronic, mechanical,
photocopying, recording or otherwise without the prior permission of
Landmark Publishing Ltd.

British Library Cataloguing in Publication Data: a catalogue record for this book is
available from the British Library.

Print: MPG Ltd, Bodmin, Cornwall
Design: Mark Titterton
Cover by James Allsopp

Front cover: Mill Lane, Oakamoor
Back cover Top: The Cock Inn, Elkstones
Back cover Middle: Cheddleton, taken pre 1920
Back cover Bottom: The outflow from New Pool
(Tittesworth Reservoir), in Edwardian times

Contents

Introduction

The bulk of these photographs are from the collection of Lindsey Porter. Many fall into two parts: those which pre-date the Second World War and photos taken by his maternal uncle, the late Arthur Goldstraw after the war. It was he who taught his nephew the rudiments of photography and some of those used are taken by him as a result. Nearly all of them, and those supplied by others, have something in common: they record scenes which no longer exist – portraying a way of life or buildings which are no longer extant.

Some parts of the Staffordshire Moorlands and the Churnet Valley – we have defined the area very loosely – have changed significantly. The Churnet Valley used to be heavily industrialised, but much of this has now gone – although traces of some of it may be found relatively easily.

The character of much of Dovedale has changed too, although this has already been covered in detail by Lindsey Porter in "Bygone Days in Dovedale and the Manifold Valley". Despite instances such as these, many of the photographs did not carry a uniform theme and so much of this book consists of many diverse scenes simply listed under the village in which they were taken. However, this diversity has added significantly to the interest of this book. Many of the changes are subtle, but looking at the book as a whole, it's amazing how we have moved on.

Lindsey Porter has recently published Victorian Times In and Around Ashbourne: Photographs from the Nineteenth Century. It contains many views which complement some subjects found in this book. These include some of the country houses close to Ashbourne, such as Alton Towers, Calwich Abbey, Wootton Hall, Ilam Hall (including a sequence of scenes showing the interior), Dovedale, Mayfield and Ellastone – all in North Staffordshire.

Some of the scenes to be found in these pages have been reproduced before. However, we took a conscious decision to include them here. This was because they had previously appeared as small images in Staffordshire Moorlands: Pictures from the Past, or where technological advances has meant that the originals can now be reproduced to a much higher quality. It seemed a shame not to give them another airing on this basis.

This book contains some 316 photographs. Clearly it is only a representative sample of the photos which must be resting in albums in drawers all over the Moorlands and beyond. However, most of these are not from poorish quality postcards but from high quality lantern slides and 35 mm originals; we hope our selection keeps you interested as you turn the pages.

Some of the captions have drawn on material published elsewhere. "Pevsner" refers to The Buildings of England: Staffordshire by N Pevsner and 'VCH' refers to The Victoria County History: Vol VII, Leek and the Moorlands, rediculously priced at £70.

Our thanks are due to the following for providing photographs (in alphabetical order):

Tom Buxton, John Davey, John Ellis, David Gordon, Yvonne Goldstraw, Robert Gratton, Adrian Henstock, Leek Post and Times, Jim Plant, Staffordshire County Library Service (Leek), the late J W Walker, G W Walwyn.

We are conscious that some of the photographs we have used were taken by talented photographers with limited equipment a hundred or so years ago. Amongst these was WH Nithsdale in particular and it is appropriate that he should not be forgotten.

The areas covered exclude the towns of Leek, Biddulph and Cheadle. We wanted this book to be about the rural part of the district. We are producing two volumes of photos on Leek in the 20th Century and a book on Biddulph has recently been published elsewhere. We hope our arbitrary decision finds approval.

Lindsey Porter and Cathryn Walton

Horton Hall, built in the 17th Century and photographed about one hundred years ago in this scene. The sash windows were added after the house was built, but seem to add to the charm of this lovely old building. The first house outside London to have sash windows was Chatsworth House in around 1690

Swythamley Hall, the home of the Brocklehurst family until the death of Sir Philip Brocklehurst. The house was auctioned off (along with the rest of the Swythamley estate) and became a transcendental meditation centre, later reverting back to a home. The Hall replaced a previous house destroyed by fire in 1813 (Pevsner). Here a herd of deer grazes by the west front

This coach must have been a 'one off'. It incorporated designs of other, more common coaches, but also had some unusual characteristics, which may indicate that it was built by a local craftsman. It is seen at Swythamley Hall

Many local country seats had a herd of deer – Wootton Lodge still has them – and we have seen a photo of them at Swythamley, see page 8. These are in Ashcombe Park, Cheddleton, and there was another herd at Okeover Park

Cliffe Park Hall, Rudyard, photographed during its days as a youth hostel. It had accommodation for 80 people and closed its doors on 7th December 1969. It has previously been a golf club run by the North Staffordshire/LMS Railway between 1906 and 1926. Pevsner states that it was built circa 1830, but it is known to be some 20 years older. It is situated on the west side of Rudyard Lake

Another country seat, which has also opened its doors to the public, is Swainsley Hall in the Maniford Valley. It was built in 1867 as a summer home for Richard Roscoe, a London solicitor. He was probably introduced to the area by his wife who was the grand-daughter of John Taylor, a Cornishman, who was appointed manager of the adjacent Ecton Mine by the Duke of Devonshire in 1818.

For many years it was owned by the daughter of Sir Thomas Wardle. The latter had purchased the house from Roscoe. She was married to Admiral Sir Guy Gaunt and the house was known as Gaunts Wood for a while. In the 1950s, it was sold and used as a public house for a time. This photograph dates from about 1920

Basford Hall, the home of John Sneyd. Three of his sons occupied estates in this area: Ashcombe, Basford and Belmont. This photograph dates from the early years of the 20th Century. The house is still occupied by one of John Sneyd's descendants. In the 19th Century it was the home of Susannah Ingleby, whose diary has recently been published

Throwley Hall in 1910. A proposal to turn it into a hotel failed; it might have been its saviour had it succeeded. It is situated west of Ilam high above the Manifold Valley. The property has deteriorated significantly since this photograph was taken, although the ruins have now been stabilised

Another ruin: the west wing of Beresford Hall, above Beresford Dale, in 1857. It was the intention of Mr Beresford-Hope, the owner of the Beresford Estate, to rebuild the house, but his intention was never realised, although the house was pulled down in 1858 in anticipation of the rebuilding. The roof of part of the house had collapsed by 1836, but the south front (see over) remained 'in tolerable order'

The Fishing Temple of Charles Cotton and Izaak Walton, built in 1674. The trees have now gone. The foreground used to be a bowling green, but all signs of this have gone too. See also the photo on page 149

Alton Towers, once the home of the Earl of Shrewsbury, is portrayed in this group of photographs (overleaf), which include the garden in all its glory. The house is now virtually a shell

The Stables, covered in ivy

The view towards The Conservatory. The lion may now be seen outside the council offices in Leek

These lovely gates must have been sold, for they no longer exist. If they survive on the estate, their restoration seems long overdue

Some of the statues and urns which adorned this immaculately kept garden

The Swiss Cottage from across the valley. Perversely, it was originally occupied by a harpist who played in the huge entrance hall of the house. A blind person was employed who could not enjoy the scene from the Cottage

Calwich Abbey, built in 1846-49 and demolished in 1935. It was built by Augustus Duncombe, whose name is remembered at the Duncombe Arms, in nearby Ellastone. Here is the West front with the main entrance

Wootton Hall, also demolished in the 1930s

One of the pair of "Milanese Gates", as they were known, at the drive entrance to Wootton Hall. They may be seen at Capesthorne Hall, the surviving home of the Bromley-Davenport family, near Macclesfield

Three views of Biddulph Old Hall, taken about 100 years ago. It was destroyed during the Civil War. Pevsner describes it as late 17th Century

This is Birdsgrove House, perhaps little known to most North Staffordshire people. It is tucked away behind trees and bushes on the A52 by the turning for Okeover. When this photograph was taken early in the 20th Century, it was the home of the Wright family but is now a private residential centre

The Roaches House. The top floor has now been removed. The house was originally part of the Swythamley estate and was built in 1876 (VCH, p.194). It is situated at the south eastern end of Hen Cloud on The Roaches

Two views of Rock Cottage, which is partly excavated out of the rock known as Five Clouds on The Roaches. A cave at the southern end of The Roaches was inhabited in the 17th Century and was known as Rockhall in 1770, (VCH, p194). This was incorporated into this house. In 1872 Princess Mary, Duchess of Teck, was entertained here. A seat was cut out of the rock above, so that she could admire the view (see page 182). The house remained occupied until 1989

The ruins of Ashenhurst Mill, Bradnop (on the right of the photograph), with the mill house on the left. The mill ceased working in the mid 1880s (VCH, p174), but the substantial Mill House survives

Ashenhurst Mill House in the 1890s

Ashenhurst Hall stables in the autumn. The Hall (below) was demolished in 1954 and the stables have since been converted to a dwelling

Chapter 2 – Winter Wonderland

Our moorlands receive their fair share of snow as we all know. Here are a few scenes of several past winters.

The winter of 1947. Leaving Bottom House for Leek on 15th February 1947

Spicer Stone Farm, Leekbrook, early in the 20th Century

A slide in the snow entertained these girls outside their school near Ramshaw Rocks on the Leek - Buxton road

The scene above is of Waterhouses Station, showing the narrow gauge train. The photograph must pre-date 1913, for the loco's coal bunker had been heightened by then and this photograph shows it prior to the alteration. The signal is on the NSR standard gauge line

Cheddleton Wharf dusted with snow. The right hand narrowboat (not called a barge) is laden and low in the water. It is heading up towards Froghall and one wonders what it is carrying. Prior to 1890, when the Whiston Smelter closed, cargoes of copper ore (from Coniston and overseas) came down the canal system to Froghall Wharf, bound for Whiston from Liverpool. Alternatively, it may have been coal from The Potteries

Heading for Thorncliffe Bank. The hill must have been difficult to ascend in icy weather with a horse and cart, especially a loaded one

The Lumb Farm, with the Mermaid Inn further up the road and with Scope Farm beyond that. The latter was a small holding with a couple of fields north of the Warslow Road. Both farms have now been demolished. The name Lumb must be associated with a vein called The Lum(b), which existed at Royledge Copper Mine, east of Lumb Farm. The vein ranged in the general direction of Lumb Farm, but had probably petered out before reaching this area. A gate post is the sole survivor of the place

In February 1895, the Leek Fire Brigade gained immortality locally when they attended a fire at Rudyard Lake. The fire was below the road at the lakeside and the intrepid fire crew lowered their tender through the wood to the frozen surface of the lake, where they attacked the fire. Rather than haul the tender back up through the wood, the horses were taken down and the crew returned to Rudyard down the frozen surface of the lake. The ice is reported to have been 18 inches thick. The fire crew were: **Back row:** J L Jones, T Allcock, E Hughes, J Billing, H Billing, H Buxton **Middle row:** R Carding, A J Halton, J Carding, A Carding, Sec. W B Nadin, Captn. A H Wardle. **Front row:** Dr P H V Hammersley, Lieut. H Foster, W Willshaw

Winter used to be much harsher than today and skating on ice was a common pastime. Records survive describing skating on the River Churnet at Oakamoor for instance in c.1880 (above the mill pool). It comes as no surprise that the frozen surface of Rudyard Lake attracted many visitors (above), although what was intended with the bikes is unclear! These photographs are from a postcard dated 1908. The cyclist on the left is Ethan Porter

The River Churnet at Oakamoor weir, by the road bridge. The building on the left is the Old Police House. The villas at the top of the photo are now difficult to see from the bridge because of trees

Houses at the rear of The Cricketers pub. The terrace stretches between the pub and Jimmy's Yard and runs parallel to the former canal between Froghall and Uttoxeter. Just off the photograph on the right, the old canal bridge (which carried the road over the canal and is now blocked up) can still be seen. The canal closed in 1846!

A snowy scene at Oakamoor Railway Station, looking towards the tunnel and Froghall, early in the 20th Century

Jimmy's Yard, Oakamoor

Caught in the snow in the 1947 winter between Leek and Bottom House. This photograph was taken on 15th February. Note the telephone wires which now run underground. The following photographs are also dated 1947

The snow lasted for many weeks. A mercy flight on 8th February to Butterton in a Halifax plane ended in disaster when it crashed on Grindon Moor. It was thought that the pilot believed he was higher than he actually was

(Above left): This is thought to be Solomons Hollow in 1947. *(Above right):* H S Goldstraw with ice-encrusted telephone wires on the road to Onecote

The view from Cooks Hollow near Lowe Hill Bridge towards Poolhall, near Bradnop

George Mason's van heading for Leek

The crossroads above Bottom House on the road to Onecote showing the road to Morredge (above) and damage to telephone wires (below)

The original George Inn in Waterhouses. It is now the Olde Beams restaurant and the barn on the right has been removed

These two adjacent pubs in Ellastone recalled the two local aristocratic families – the Duncombe Arms (right) and Bromley Arms (with the steps). The Duncombes lived at Calwich Abbey, which they rebuilt in the 1840s. The Bromley-Davenports owned nearby Wootton Hall. The Bromley Arms is now a private house

The former Navigation Inn at Froghall, adjacent to the canal tunnel. The building has now been demolished. The photograph was taken in 1974

The Cock Inn at Upper Elkstones in Edwardian times. The landlord was John Bradbury. The village's domestic water came from a spring behind the photographer. It looks as though the young girl, with the yoke, was on her way there after this photograph was taken. See also page 65

Another view of the The Cock Inn, kept by Redvers Cooper. This photo was taken in the early 1960s. The village has since lost its school, pub and shop. The pub closed in 1976. It was in existence in 1816 (VCH, p57)

The Fountain Inn, Meerbrook. It was eventually demolished when the "New Pool" – Tittesworth Reservoir – was extended between 1959-62. A new road is being built at the rear of the pub. It involved a new bridge to carry the road over the new water level. The pub was existing in 1834 (VCH, p 193)

Another view of the Inn. The landlord was L Sheldon

The other Meerbrook pub, taken in the early 1960s, when it kept its more appropriate name of the The Three Horseshoes. Three horse shoes may be seen hanging from the end of the building. The licensee was Ernest Belfield. In 1818, it was The Horseshoe, but was the Three Horseshoes in 1834 (VCH, p193). It is now The Lazy Trout. It is a pity that historic names are lost in this way

The former Blacksmiths Arms at Bradnop, after being destroyed by fire in c. 1940. It is now a dwelling house. The fire appears to have completely gutted the building. The pub was opposite the lane to Ashenhurst Hall and was in use in around 1850 (VCH, p170)

In the 1950s, following the death of Lady Gaunt, Swainsley Hall was sold and opened its doors as a pub. It reopened as a restaurant a few years ago but is now a private house again

The Shoulder of Mutton, Grindon, which changed its name to The Cavalier

The Golden Lion Inn, formerly a Joules house in Ipstones. The pub is now called The Linden Tree. The village has not only lost the name of an old inn, this rural lane is now the main road through the village

Joules was a good brew made in Stone, near Stafford. Taken over by Bass, they moved the brewing to Burton and closed down the brewery. Here is the Marquis of Granby in Ipstones and Alexander's grocery shop on the left

The Black Lion Inn, Butterton. George Goodwin was the licensee when this photograph was taken in the early 1960s. All his beers were drawn straight from the barrel. They were kept on a stillage at the rear of the room to the right of the door. After he retired, the pub was extended on the right hand side to the rear. It is now a popular country hostelry serving drinks, food and offering accommodation

The Izaak Walton Hotel

Dovedale

Photographed in 1903, after the Prince family had left to open the Ashbourne Hall Hotel in 1900. It was part of the Ilam Hall estate until 1875 when the Watts-Russell family sold up. It now belongs to the Duke of Rutland

This photograph dates from 1868. The inn opened in 1851 as the Rudyard Lake Hotel. The house had previously been the home of the bailiff of the North Staffordshire Railway Company, whose line opened here in 1849

The hotel following alterations to the building and the name

The Royal Cottage, by the Buxton-Leek road at Middle Hills. It is built on the side of a road which post-dates the 1745 rebellion of Bonnie Prince Charlie, with whom the inn is supposed to be linked. The landlord was Eli S Brunt in 1909, about the time this photograph was taken

The Red Lion, Cheddleton. The petrol pump, shop and forge have now gone, but the pub of course remains at the bottom of the hill to Wetley Rocks

The Crewe and Harpur Arms Hotel Longnor. It was built with bricks made at nearby Reapsmoor. To the right is the road to Warslow

The Grouse Inn, Warslow. Isaac Birch ran this pub from October 1853 and he was still there at the end of 1871. Later the inn became a temperance establishment between 1900 and 1904 (VCH, p57). The Grouse probably became the name when Isaac Birch took it over. It was previously called The Crewe & Harpur Arms

Two Burmese servants at Farley Hall. They were brought back by Charles Bill. They must have cut a dash in sartorial style if nothing else. One wonders what happened to them and whether they ever returned home. Colonel Bill served in Burma with the North Staffordshire Regiment during 1886. He was awarded the Indian Frontier Medal for his role in the annexation of Northern Burma

The Farm

This and the next few pages show views on the farm. This ploughman would no doubt be pleased with his straight furrows

Harrowing fields the hard way

An early horse drawn mowing machine

This photograph dates from the 1950s and the general view is towards Hen Cloud and The Roaches. This traditional heavy barrow was in common use, little changed in design, for generations. It was sometimes called a 'trundle'. The design appears on several photographs in this book. One of the authors (LP) with Len Kirkham and Peter Thompson located one in the Royledge Copper Mine near the Mermaid Inn recently. The mine closed in 1858, but the barrow was still in good condition. It was removed for preservation at the Peak District Mining Museum, Matlock Bath prior to the mine being closed again

Pitching the hay into the hay loft after it had been collected in. This photograph was probably taken near to Longnor. The opening in the wall was called a 'pitching hole'. Note the prop taking the weight off the shaft for the benefit of the horse

Pitching hay at Hardings Booth, near Longnor. This man could never have foreseen today's big bales and the huge tractors that make their transportation look easy

This scene epitomises much that has been lost on our farms, although some farmers are finding that a switch to organic production techniques may be more profitable. This "free range" pig sleeps in the summer sun at Pheasants Clough Farm, Upperhulme

Mr Thomas Smith of Carder Green sharpening his scythe

(Above): Ringing a pig at Wetton. This was necessary with boars, which were taken to various farms to sire a new litter, or for taking them to market, etc

(Left): Walking a pig prior to motor transport near Thorncliffe. This one has not been ringed and the string is tied to the pig's leg

End of the day! Mr George Slack of Crowdecote relaxes with his clay pipe by a dry stone wall. Notice the copers, held in position with lime mortar, on the top of the wall

Meadow Farm, Crowdecote with Mrs Horobin by the wall. This probably dates from around 100 years ago and the farm must have been one of the last in the area to have a thatched roof

Mrs Horobin outside Meadow Farm

Telegrams: MANIFOLD DAIRY. LONGNOR.

SHEEN, ... 193

NEAR BUXTON.

.. 𝔇r. to the ..

Manifold Valley Dairy Association
LIMITED.

Secretary: W. H. SHIRLEY, REWLACH. SHEEN, BUXTON.

Date.			cwts.	qrs.	lbs.	Rate	£	s.	d.

A blank invoice from the cheese factory at Reapsmoor. This was a farmers' co-operative originally making Derby cheeses, having been established in the 1870s. In 1936, it was sold to Express Dairies Ltd., who made Cheddar, Cheshire and Caerphilly cheeses as well as Derby. Despite being extended in 1948, production ended in 1950 (*Industrial Archaeology of the Peak District*, H Harris, p 155). The Express Dairy name board was still on the building in the 1970s (see below). See also pp76-77 for scenes of the Ecton cheese factory. There were three others in the Moorlands: Hopedale, near Alstonfield; plus Hartington and Glutton Bridge (both actually on the Derbyshire bank of the River Dove)

This forge at Pool End, near Rudyard, operated for some 300 years before finally closing 20-30 years ago. In this photograph, and overleaf, we see the blacksmith reshoeing a horse

This scene is in Longnor. Notice the barrow, already observed on other photographs in this book. A horse and cart stands ready behind the two horses having their photograph taken

Going home on Biddulph Moor. This was a rare sight in the early 1960s when this photograph was taken

A timeless scene, driving cattle down the lane. This scene is at Cheddleton in the 1950s

(Above left): Mr George Tunnicliffe of Queen Street, Longnor, off to fetch water. *(Above right):* Joshua Millward, a Longnor based auctioneer for nearly half a century from the early 1870s

Queuing at the travelling shop in Longnor's Market Place

Mr Sykes, the Longnor Cobbler, repairing a boot

Mr Sykes clearly had more interest in his cello than in tidying his cobbler's shop! In fact, he was a keen musician and was also the chapel organist. His son Herbert took over the business

The telegraph man at Butterton Ford. However, the children seem more fascinated with the camera!

The yokes have gone, but the buckets still needed to be filled at this tap in Upper Elkstones, situated above the school and Grove Cottage. The tap no longer exists. This photo dates from the early 1960s

The view across the mill pond at Oakamoor in 1933. The site of the works is now a country park

W H Nithsdale of Leek took this photograph of the Oakamoor Copper Works and called it "Smokeamoor"!
The local Environmental Health Officer would have a field day now if this occurred. Bolton's must have been
burning some poor quality coal

Aerial views of the Oakamoor Works. Here the copper core of the first successful transatlantic cable was manufactured in 1856

An early view of the Oakamoor works and the cottages in Mill Lane. It was taken in the 1860s. All the buildings in the foreground have gone, including all the houses in Mill Lane

Three views of the interior of the Oakamoor works. They were taken in 1946. This is a hydraulic tube piecer

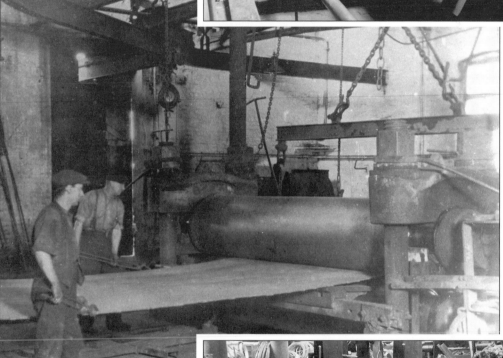

(Above): Rolling sheet copper/brass

(Left): An old strip rolling machine

Working on a barrow-run across the River Churnet during a dry spell at Oakamoor

Derailed goods wagons caused the damage which resulted in these men working to repair the line in 1886 at the junction of the sidings to Bolton's works, at Oakamoor. Beyond is the railway tunnel. It was a quarter of a mile and 22 yards long. This was important to the platelayers who earned more money because of that 22 yards!

The Whiston Copper Smelter, which closed in 1890

Cheddleton Flint Mill, with both wheels turning, from an old lantern slide. There were many watermills in the area, but two wheels adjacent to each other was rare generally and the only local example

Cherry Eye Mine's wharf near Froghall. Its name relates to the colour of the dust from the ore which presumably collected on the miners' faces. The narrow boat is being loaded with bright red iron ore. The mine closed c.1923. It was on the north side of the canal and was the area's last ironstone mine

This viaduct enabled iron ore to be brought down the canal from Kingsley Far Banks. There was a substantial development of iron ore mining in the 19th Century around here. The Woodhead Company's tramway viaduct was built in c.1860 and lasted until 1887. A similar structure existed at Apes Tor, Ecton, in the Manifold Valley, but was an aqueduct. That existed between 1823 and c.1856. *(Below):* The central span of the viaduct over the River Churnet. The one-legged man is William Sargeant, agent of Eli Bowers, who owned the Woodhead Company, which worked the adjacent estate for ironstone

Miners at the Ecton Copper Mine c.1884. The tramway on the left brought ore from Salts Level, situated behind the copper-spired building on the hillside (built after the mine closed). The ore (in the heap in the foregound) was reduced to fine sand and separated from the rock and spar in water. The circular pits on the right (known as buddles) were part of this process. They were purchased second hand in Cornwall

Another view of the Ecton dressing floor. Tubs from the Clayton Mine (situated at the roadside and just above river level) were hauled up the hillside on a wooden incline by a steam engine situated in the two storey building. The tubs passed through the building and down onto the dressing floor

The entrance to the Ecton mine. This replaced the original level (which started in 1723) in 1774. The original 1723 lessees (who included some speculators from the Leek area) gave up when the money ran out. However, some persevered with a new lease in 1739 and soon discovered the rich deposit of copper ore which made the mine so famous

Remains of the Waterbank lead and zinc mine on Ecton Hill. It closed in 1889. The building is a 'coe' and contained a climbing shaft into the mine. This photograph may predate the activities here of the Ecton Co. Ltd. which started work in 1883

Two views of the Ecton Creamery and Cheese Factory. It opened in 1919 and was operated by F W Gilbert Ltd., of Derby. It utilised old mine buildings and had a siding linked to the Manifold Light Railway. It was later sold to Wilts United Dairies and closed in 1933

At the road side, employees at the Ecton Creamery pose for a photograph on the unloading area for milk churns

A close up of the Creamery. Unfortunately it is slightly out of focus. The mine entrance is the one on p.75 having been extended so that the Light Railway's track could be brought above it

Reconstruction of the cement works at Cauldon Low. The road had still to be widened. This works was subsequently rebuilt by Blue Circle a few years ago

Part of the quarry complex at Cauldon Low of what used to be Derbyshire Stone's works in the 1960s

Several of the former Cauldon Low Quarries were abandoned in 1920 when the line to Froghall closed. The Leek Field Club made a survey of the quarries, listing the flora and fauna which had become established there. Despite the haven it had become, it now lies under many feet of quarry waste. Here is the former railway line into the quarry

Tramlines ran to the quarry face and here men toiled to load wagons with stone. The waste accumulated at the side of the tracks creating the undulating appearance seen here. It was thirsty work and the men are recorded as drinking a gallon of beer each lunch time, four pints before tea and another gallon afterwards

This tunnel ran through to another large quarry face – Dunkirk Quarry

This scene is of one of several truncated domes which dotted the western side of the old quarry. They contained lime. Limestone, layered with timber, was covered with turf and burnt. For some reason, the resultant lime was never recovered

A youthful looking Lindsey Porter examines some of the lime uncovered below the turf in 1963 from one of the 'domes'

The Froghall works of Thomas Bolton beside the Caldon Canal. It was built in 1890, one of the two chimneys has now been demolished

The location of this steam driven crusher is unknown, but it is probably seen during construction work at Bolton's, Froghall

Three scenes of the old watermill at Froghall. The first two (right and middle) date from early in the 20th Century, the lower one from 1972. It was used as a colour mill but it has since closed. Iron ore from the Churnet Valley was ground here to make a pigment for paint. In the heyday of mining (c.1855-1864) large quantities of ore from Cherry Eye Mine was brought up the canal to Froghall Wharf. Much of the ore went to various iron works with as many as thirty narrowboats a day employed in this task, let alone railway traffic. Trade declined when the mill began to import cheaper ore from Spain

Disused flint kilns at Podmore's Mill, Consall Forge, November 1972

Remains of part of Crowgutter Mill, a former flint mill, looking towards the canal in 1972

Crowgutter Mill from the Caldon Canal towpath in November 1972. Much of the site was later to be covered with silt dredged from the canal

Brickworks were once common in the Moorlands area. There were at least three on Ashbourne Road, Leek; one at Brown Edge; and others at Wall Grange; Cellarhead; Kingsley; Rushton; Heaton and Reapsmoor (near Longnor). It is likely that there were others too. The builders of large projects, such as Alton Towers and Moor Court, near Oakamoor, made their own bricks

The abandoned Wall Grange Brickworks in 1972 and the demolition of the works chimney in 1963. It was situated to the left of the rear building

Three scenes showing the demolition of the chimney

Tatton's dyehouse at Upperhulme, after the fire in 1891 which destroyed most of the mill. In 1970, the dyeing and warping activities were transferred to Buxton Road, Leek, but another fire destroyed that mill in May 1975

This building was built as the Count House of the New York Copper Mine in 1849. It is a Cornish term and reflects the fact that the mine manager, Richard Niness, was Cornish. It is situated at the top of Hamps Valley, south of the Mermaid Inn on Morredge. The mine had a huge Cornish beam engine in a house similar to the ruined tin mine engine houses one sees all over Cornwall. The pond was the reservoir for the engine's boiler. The mine venture was a failure, however. In this context, the Count House was probably the mine office. The building has recently been demolished. This photograph is slightly out of focus.

Man-haulage was not common on the canals except on maintenance boats, such as this one, and then only over short distances. This boat, with what appears to be a cargo of sand or lime, is at Froghall by the tunnel entrance

Price and Son of Brierley Hill carried limestone to the ironworks in the Black Country. Here are two views of their boat "Nora" at Consall Forge

Several views of narrowboats plying their trade on the Caldon Canal seem to fit well into this chapter

Another narrowboat laden with limestone passes through Consall Forge. There must have been countless thousands of trips like this one

This is n.b. "Shannon", again at Consall Forge. The building in the distance was part of a tramway which climbed out of the valley to Consall, heading for Cellarhead, between 1816-1840s

This narrow boat has just left the lock at Podmore's Mill near Consall Forge. This boat is riding high, so it may be travelling empty having made a trip to Froghall, perhaps with copper ore for Whiston Smelter or supplies for Boltons. The apparatus above the horse and behind the hedge defies explanation

Passing through Cheddleton Wharf with a cargo of limestone. The horse is eating as it pulls the narrowboat. The bridge carries the main road from Leek. Beyond it, another narrowboat may be seen at the wharf

A horse plods slowly towards Froghall pulling an empty narrowboat as an uptrain passes by. The hillside scars on the right show the ironstone mine tips on Kingsley Far Banks.

A narrowboat heads into the Froghall tunnel heading for Froghall Wharf. The horse went around, which meant that the boat had to be 'legged' through, by the boatman lying on the cabin roof and using his legs to push the boat through the tunnel

The Manifold Valley Light Railway at Thor's Cave Station. The large shed was the refreshment hut, while the little building was the station shelter with two toilets behind it. The coaches of the train were initially primrose yellow. A new book of photographs of the railway has just been published: *The Leek and Manifold Valley Light Railway* by Lindsey Porter

Hulme End Station on the Manifold Line. The booking office is on the left; the engine shed is behind the water tower and on the right is the carriage shed. The booking office is now a Visitor Centre. It has a working model of the station and is well worth a visit

A NSR train at Bradnop Station heading for Waterhouses. The line opened in 1905 and the siding from where the scene was taken led to the coalyard. The line has been unused for some time but the rails are intact and renewed use to Cauldon Low Quarry is expected shortly. The waiting room has gone

A train of mixed goods wagons awaits the main line, having just come down the Waterhouses line in June 1929. The scene is at Leekbrook and the passenger train is headed by ex LNW 4-4-0 No 5357 *Bassethound*

A sand train passes Rudyard Lake headed by No 48106, a Stanier 8F 2-8-0 locomotive. The train was delivering sand from Oakamoor to Widnes

Staff at Rudyard Lake Station in 1956. The station is immaculately maintained, a credit to the men: (left to right) Percy Adams (porter); J Keeling (relief signals); W Smart (porter/signals); JE Banks (Station Master)

A sand train bound for Oakamoor waits for the Cheddleton gates alongside the track lifting gang's lorry loaded with sleepers in 1972. The gates were unlocked by the train guard who is seen ahead of the locomotive

Froghall Station, awaiting the next train in the early years of the 20th Century. Bolton's chimney may be seen in the distance

(Above): A lovely view of the crossing by Oakamoor Station. The horse, cart and dog wait patiently as NSR loco No 29 crosses tracks

(Right): The British Industrial Sand siding at Moneystones Quarry c. 1974. Photographed on a Sunday, this shipment of sand awaits collection and delivery to the Albion Bottle Company at Langley Green

Here a brakeman rides with the descending wagons towards Froghall. The incline had three rails

One of the small saddle tank locomotives which operated in the quarries at Cauldon Low, prior to the closure of the incline to Froghall in 1920. The latter was cable hauled and was replaced by the Leek – Waterhouses branch which opened in 1904 and also connected with the Manifold Valley Light Railway. The loco was built in 1877 by Hughes and Co of Loughborough

The Froghall to Cauldon incline, the third oldest tramway to be authorised by Parliament. The scene is east of the tunnel, close to the quarries. The road to Windy Arbour is on the right

The Earl of Shrewsbury takes the reins of his coach on the Alton, Cheadle, Leek, Buxton run which he originated. It was called "Greyhound". The fifty five horses used in working the route were put up for sale at Leicester on 14th October 1893 (see *The Road* 1st October 1893)

A lovely scene of a three horse coach climbing out of the dales

A horse drawn sleigh heads towards the bridge at Hulme End

Sir Vauncey Harpur-Crewe (nearest the camera) and friends about to leave his summer seat, Warslow Hall

A two-horse team waits while the owner has a chat. The cart on the right is loaded with milk churns and will be heading for the Ecton Creamery. It is outside the village shop in Warslow

Making deliveries in Warslow outside what was the Methodist Chapel. The extra horse was needed on the surrounding hills; even so, it was not possible to haul a full load of stone out of the Manifold Valley in one go. Half a load was fetched, offloaded in Warslow and the other half fetched before reloading the first half – and all done by hand of course! In this scene, the wagon is probably loaded with cattle feed

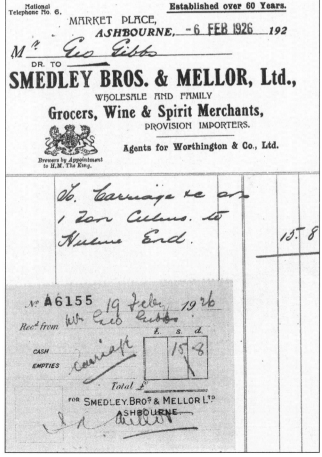

(Above): Agricultural suppliers of Leek, Ashbourne and Bakewell served the farmers of the Moorlands. This is the horse and cart of W Barnes, agricultural ironmongers and ironfounders of The Market Place, Ashbourne, who supplied agricultural machinery

(Left): Across The Market Place from Barnes' in Ashbourne was Smedley Brothers and Mellor, who also served the farmers. In this case one ton of cattle feed was being sold to Mr George Gibbs of Hulme End. Culms (or Coombes) were the waste from brewing; note that Smedley's were agents for Worthington's brewery of Burton-on-Trent

Relaxing at Knypersley Castle in the late 1950s

Sports events at Moor Court, Oakamoor

An interesting view of a child's carriage pulled by a small pony. This is also at Moor Court

Heading for Rudyard in 1893. The cyclists have just passed Rudyard Station. The railway had opened in 1849, making Rudyard Lake a popular destination for a day trip

These men are probably labourers having a break from working on loading limestone into narrowboats at Froghall Wharf. They are standing on the bridge outside the former Navigation Inn over the tunnel entrance on the Ipstones road. These men would be used to drinking a lot – their work was dehydrating and dusty

This bridge at Beeston Tor was replaced by a new road bridge in c.1903 by the Manifold Valley Light Railway as part of a settlement with Earl Cathcart who owned the Throwley Estate under a marriage settlement of 1852. This photo dates from the 1890s

The location of this photograph is unknown which is a pity. It might be in Warslow, taken from what is now the Onecote – Longnor road looking towards the road to Leek. If the two girls were in service at Warslow Hall, it would account for their attire

This is Warslow's Victoria Lodge of the Manchester Unity of Oddfellows. It was established in 1842, but was wound up in 1983. Warslow had a much larger population in the 19th Century owing to the mines in the area, all of which were active in the 1840s. Behind the banner is the village band. Established as a brass band by 1873, it became a silver band nearly 50 years ago and is still going strong (VCH p.58)

Cooling off in the River Dane at Gig Hall bridge, with the trout ladders beyond

A rope wire bridge across the River Dane. It is believed to have been upstream of Gig Hall Bridge. A further photograph survives of another one in a narrow ravine which must have been not too far away from this one

The Austin and Heath families paused for this photograph in the late 1890s at Rudyard Lake

The summer crowds surround a flock of swans near to the dam on Rudyard Lake. The building was built as the Earl of Macclesfield's boat house. Our fascination with water is undiminished. Carsington Water, east of Ashbourne, now attracts a million visitors each year

The dam at Rudyard Lake in 1913 showing another holiday crowd. See pp 176-179 for more views of this popular destination

A group of visitors by the cross in Ilam

The opening of Ilam Hall Youth Hostel on 22nd September, 1935. Holding his trilby is Lawrence Ramsbottom, unpaid YHA Regional Secretary from Derby. To his left is Robert McDougal who, at the instigation of Mr Ramsbottom, gave the building to the National Trust on condition that it was to be used for the youth of the world as a youth hostel. Next to him is George Cadbury, of the chocolate manufacturers. Also present is the Bishop of Lichfield.

Second from the right is Laurie Landon of Stoke-on-Trent who became YHA's International Committee Chairman for over 30 years. Far right is Bernard Edwards, who became YHA's first paid Regional Secretary in 1946, running the North Midlands youth hostels, including Ilam Hall. At the time, YHA called on the Government to establish a National Park in Dovedale. Aspirations grew and eventually the Peak District National Park was formed in 1951

The crowds relax at the Dovedale stepping stones in the 1950s. Half a century earlier, there were hardly any trees here. They resulted from the removal of animals from the slopes, especially sheep

The Leek Field Club at Mill Dale in 1961. This cottage no longer offers refreshments, but the long tradition is continued at a cottage across the road

Cheddleton Church from the lane to Wall Grange, photographed in Edwardian times

Meerbrook Church from an old lantern slide. It was built in the 1870s

Horton Church early in the 20th Century. The tower and north aisle are 15th Century but the chancel was rebuilt in the 16th Century

(Above): St Gabriel's Church, Rudyard. It was opened in 1905 on Whorrocks Bank Road (VCH p75). It started to slide down the hillside and had to be demolished in 1934.

(Above): Bagnall Church in c. 1893. *(Opposite):* The chapel at Cotton, built by AWN Pugin in 1846-8. It was lengthened in 1936-7 by George Drysdale and given a steeple (Pevsner)

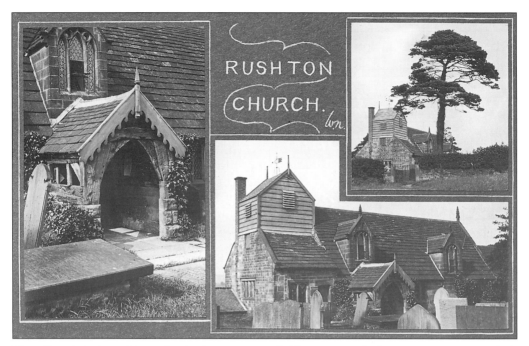

The "Church in the Wilderness" at Rushton is a remarkable survivor, which owes its presence to a lack of enthusiasm by parishoners to rebuild it on a new site in the 19th Century. Their reluctance is our undoubted gain. It has a medieval core with piecemeal alterations which have resulted in its present lack of symmetry and secular appearance. These photographs show the church in Edwardian times

The interior, from a postcard dated 1909

(Above): The view from the church to Rushton Spencer. The village has grown a lot since this was taken in the early 1960s, as well as losing its railway

(Left): This is believed to be a parish boundary stone in the churchyard. It reminds us that the church was built virtually on the boundary of Rushton James and Rushton Spencer and serves both parishes. The actual parish boundary is to the south of the church

(Above): Horton
Church lychgate,
built in 1902

(Right): The grave
of Mary Brookes at
Horton, who died
in 1787, aged 119
years

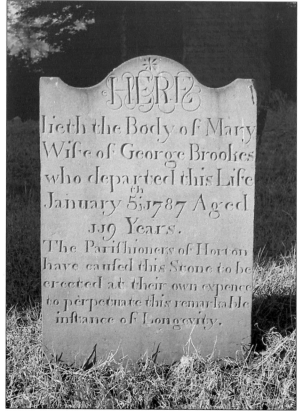

Ellastone Church from Church Lane. The pinnacles have now been removed. It has had the effect of forshortening the tower

Another view of Ellastone Church from the road to Wootton. The area to the left has been developed since this photograph was taken in 1961 with the bowling green and village hall carpark etc. The wires have also been removed!

The gates at Okeover Hall together with the 14th Century church which is now largely covered with Virginia Creeper. The gates were probably made by Benjamin Yates, who worked here between 1756-59 (Pevsner). The church has an unusual legal status, being known as a "Perculiar"

Warslow Church, built in 1820. The white gravestone is to David Martin. He was Cornish and worked at the nearby Dale Lead Mine in the 19th Century. Traditionally, it is held locally that his last wish was that he be buried as near to his native Cornwall as was possible. Although he occupies the corner of the old churchyard nearest to Cornwall, one cannot help thinking that he had somewhere closer in mind!

Hollinsclough Chapel, built by John Lomas in 1801. He was a jaggerman – a packhorse man – which reminds us that the lane coming down the hill and past his house (to the right of the chapel) was a packhorse road in former times

Chapel House, Belmont, near Ipstones before it was renovated. It was built by John Sneyd of Belmont Hall after he fell out with the vicar of Ipstones. Its low tower and east window survive

Ramsor Chapel, now demolished

This photograph of Croxden Abbey is from a group, one of which is dated 1893. Although west of the Churnet Valley, they seemed worthy of inclusion. (above and overleaf)

Alton

Alton Station, designed by AWN Pugin, fell into disrepair after the railway closed on 4th January 1965. It was restored by the Landmark Trust and this view shows the work in progress early in the 1970s. Other stations on the line were designed by W Sugden who settled in Leek and commenced his architect's practice there

Dimmingsdale, between Alton and Oakamoor, has several lakes. In the 18th Century the mill was used as a lead smelter which was later converted to a water mill. One wonders whether the Earl of Shrewsbury added more lakes for aesthetic purposes when he built the Earl's Drive, a private road which went most of the way to Cheadle. The cottage on the right has been demolished but the round house on the extreme left survives

The Dimmingsdale watermill. The mill machinery was in the left hand building. Hidden in the trees is the Earl's Drive

The view from Alton Towers Lodge towards Alton Castle. The latter was built to a design by AWN Pugin, but to the right of it, substantial remains of the Norman Castle may still be seen (but not in this photograph). The old mill by the bridge in the middle of this view is now empty. It was formerly a slitting mill, cutting up sheet brass into long thin pieces which were used as currency in Africa as part of the slave trade. Slag at the rear of the mill would seem to indicate that smelting took place here too.

The railway passed under the road in the foreground, with steps leading down to the station off to the right. Over the wall on the right, you can look down onto the overgrown mill pond. It is narrow and very long having been extended to compensate for the railway track running through part of it. In the days of the railway, this area would have been very busy with visitors to Alton Towers. The station had three platforms to accommodate the visitors and it was not unknown for all three to be in use at the same time. Now the visitors crawl up the hill in their cars to gain access to the theme park

Butterton

The ford in 1957. It has now been concreted, but one wonders if it was really necessary

The village from the Grindon Road. This was improved by the Duke of Devonshire and was used for the transportation of copper ore from the Ecton Mine to the smelter at Whiston. It became known as the Duke's New Road, but is now called Pothooks Lane

This view of the bridge north of Swainsley tunnel in the Manifold Valley has changed significantly. The bridge to the left of the road carried the trains and has now gone. The road, which seems to be less well wooded now, gave access to Butterton Station. The next time someone tells you that you cannot grow rhododendrons on limestone, send them to this station!

Cauldon Low

THE ARCH OF STALACTITES, CAULDON LOW CAVE.
(Waterhouses Station, North Stafford Railway.)

During 1906, a large cave was found at Cauldon Low Quarry. It was called the Fairy Cave and opened to the public, becoming quite a tourist attraction over two seasons before being closed. The official line is that it was quarried away, but an old quarryman assured me (LP) that it had still survived and that he could show me where the steps to it descended from the surface. The North Staffordshire Railway published three postcards of the cave, which are reproduced here. The stalactites were up to six feet long. *(Right):* This stalagmite was two feet high

INTERIOR OF CAULDON LOW CAVE.
(Waterhouses Station, North Stafford Railway.)

A PERFECT STALAGMITE. CAULDON LOW CAVE
(Waterhouses Station, North Stafford Railway.)

Cheddleton

This was taken before 1920 and shows limestone piled high on the wharf. The road was later widened over the canal

Cheddleton Wharf. The two narrowboats (right and centre) are seen with an ice breaker (left) which was permanently moored here. The building behind and right of the bridge used to be a brewery. It even used to bottle Guinness

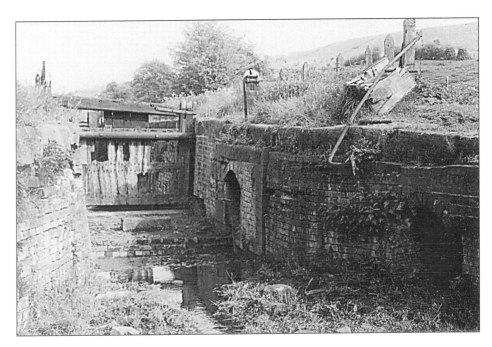

By 1972 when these photographs at Cheddleton Locks were taken, the Caldon Canal was derelict. Fortunately, The Caldon Canal Society successfully campaigned for its restoration. The work cost £57,000 and was completed in 1974. The work included: rebuilding Waterworks Lock at Stockton Brook; major work on three locks at Hazlehurst; rebuilding the sides of the two Cheddleton Locks, plus hydraulically geared gates and restoration of the boat pound between them; a new concrete channel near Froghall where there had been a landslip; and repairwork on the tunnel. Additionally, hundreds of tons of silt was removed and the Society spent countless hours cutting back bushes, undergrowth etc. The boom in leisure related activity came in the nick of time to save this valuable amenity. See *Leek Post & Times* 25/10/1973, and scenes under Froghall and Longsdon in this section

The Flint Mill in the 1950s

The village prior to the development of the two large estates either side of the main road beyond the church

Nineteenth Century stocks below the church wall and opposite the Black Lion Inn. Another pair of metal stocks exist at Warslow. Many villages would have had a pair of stocks; Longnor had a new pair made as late as 1861 (VCH p45)

The Bunting at Wetley Rocks, just south of Cheddleton, in the early 1960s

The former Churnet Valley line north of Cheddleton, at Leek Brook

Consall

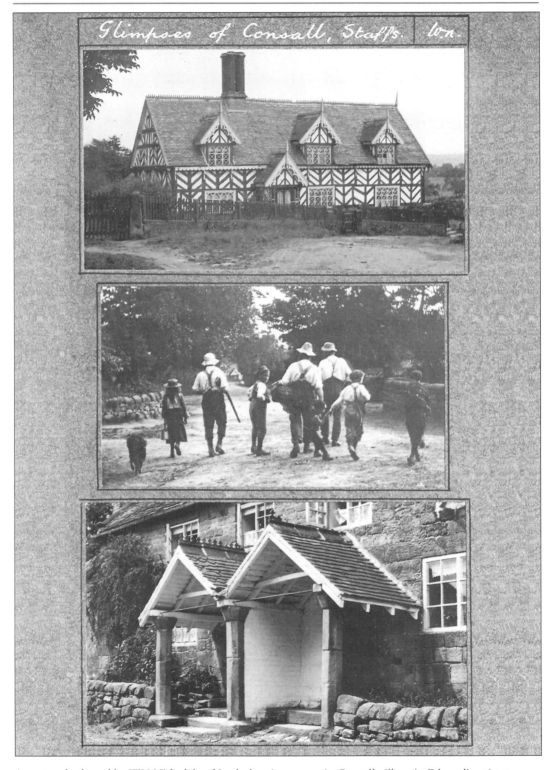

Glimpses of Consall, Staffs. WH.

A postcard released by WH Nithsdale of Leek showing scenes in Consall village in Edwardian times

A classic view of tranquility at Consall Forge. The mid-17th Century forge must have been close to the area beyond the narrow boat and between the canal and river (the river is canalised in the foreground). Before dredging operations deposited tons of silt in that area, it was possible to pick up pieces of iron slag there

This postcard was mailed on Christmas Eve, 1908 showing Consall Forge

Consall Forge, showing cottages in the foreground which have now been demolished. The Black Lion is off to the right and the site of the cottages is now used for parking

A view of the Churnet Valley and London Bridge from Kingsley Far Banks. The cottages have gone now. The bridge was built to span the river and canal by the Consall Mineral Company, known locally as the 'London Company'. It worked coal from pits near Consall

A rare 'haystack' boiler from a Newcomen Engine in use as a water tank at Podmore's Mill, Consall Forge. It may now be seen at Cheddleton Flint Mill. This photograph was taken in 1972

Consall Forge in the early 1960s. The photograph is deceiving — this is the river in the foreground and the canal is between the people and the house

A view of The Devil's Staircase at Consall Forge in Edwardian times

Dane Valley

The Hanging Stone near Dane Bridge on the Swythamley Estate. There are fewer trees now surrounding the stone. The plaque commemorates the loss of a favourite dog

'Lady Lud' which stood at the north end of Lud Church near Gradbach. It eventually rotted away, having been erected in the 1860s and was replaced with the figurehead of the the *SS Swythamley* which is understood to have survived until the 1950s

The River Dane was impounded at Gig Hall to provide a supply of water for Rudyard Lake. It reached there via 'The Feeder'. The lake provided water for the Trent & Mersey Canal system

Taken in the 1950s, this shows that an ingenious system for supporting the bridge had been introduced using two steel wires slung beneath the bridge

The trout ladders, Gig Hall Bridge. The cottage is now reached by a road from Heaton

The Feeder supplying water to Rudyard Lake from Gig Hall Bridge weir. This scene is now very overgrown and hardly recognisable. It is taken from west of the road to Barleigh Ford Farm and the Scout camp

Flash

The Leek – Buxton road near Flash, with Oliver Hill far right

Dovedale and Ilam

(Above): The view at Lin Dale where the Stepping Stones are now situated. The river bank is now lined with alder trees. The date of installation of the Stepping Stones is unknown. *(Below):* The view back towards Lin Dale and the Stepping Stones (which are out of sight). These views are about 100 years old

This is tranquil Beresford Dale. The tree cover made it dark in places but Dutch Elm Disease devastated the timber and changed the character of the dale for ever

This remarkable photograph shows the ruins of Milldale Mill. It was a paint mill – i.e. one used for grinding red or yellow iron ore. This was mined locally and mixed with distemper to create red or yellow paint, hence the name paint mill. By the late 1870s it had closed (VCH p19). For information on the mill, see *Copper and Lead Mines Around the Manifold Valley* by L Porter and JA Robey. This is the only known photo of the mill although another survives of the end of the building

Ilam Church before it became hidden by trees. Other, older, photographs show the churchyard open to the lawn in front of the Hall, creating the appearance that the church was almost part of the garden

Having lost its top in the 1962 gales, this cross at Ilam has deteriorated significantly because of acid rain. Today, the carvings and small statues have become seriously eroded. At the time of going to print, a scheme has been announced to conserve what is left of the monument. It is good to see that this old friend is now to receive attention. However, the plans do not include the restoration of the weathered stone. What utter nonsense; nothing other than a full restoration is surely required

Dunwood from Endon before housing development started in the fields on the right

The well in Endon. The village has been dressing its well since 1845. It is one of the oldest to do so and has been dressing its well for longer than most Derbyshire villages

The well dressed in 1961. Income from the festivities at well dressing time is used to support local organisations

The village ford also in 1961

The River Hamps at Ford, looking towards the Old Hall. Taken by WH Nithsdale

Fording the River Hamps at Ford. Although a wooden bridge existed here in 1621, there wasn't one when this photograph was taken. The current bridge would appear to have been erected in Victorian times. The Old Hall is on the left

Back O Th Brook

Another ford at Brook Cottage, at Back O Th Brook, near Waterfall, in the late 1950s. Note the stepping stones, still there, but largely hidden in vegetation now. The road has since been sealed with tar, and the milk stand and road side building have gone

Froghall

(Above left): Froghall Wharf lying derelict before restoration breathed life into the area in 1974. *(Above right):* Repair work in the tunnel at Froghall in 1973 enabled this photograph to be taken

The Caldon Canal at Froghall with a narrow boat lying submerged in the water. It needed a lot of vision to restore the waterway to its present state

Gradbach

Gradbach Mill in use as a barn. It was converted to a Youth Hostel opening in 1980. It was built in 1792 by the Dakeyne family and operated as a flax and silk mill. The wheel was within the structure, at the far end and was overshot. The leat to the wheel may still be seen at the rear of the mill, but is now dry. The chimney pots are made of stone

(left): The drive to the mill showing the old lodging house.

(below): The former lodging house, which has now been demolished

Doublers Row, workers' cottages at the side of the River Dane, just upstream from the mill. This photograph was taken in 1958 and the one below in 1982. The cottages are on the Cheshire bank of the river

The belated official opening of the Youth Hostel in June 1984 by Mr Bill Banton (speaking at the mike). Behind him is John Whittington, Regional Chairman YHA Peak Region. Immediately right of the door are David Allison, Peak Regional Secretary; Hedley Alcock, YHA National Chairman and Lindsey Porter, YHA National Vice-Chairman standing together. Since the opening, over 175,000 people have stayed here. The entrance hall used to be part of the wheel pit

Gradbach Youth Hostel today, serving the needs of country lovers and preserving an historic mill into the bargain. This scene is from the packhorse way to Wildboarclough

Grindon

The road to Weags Bridge before the ugly telegraph poles were removed

Weags Barn was a familiar landmark above Weags Bridge on the road from Grindon. It was on the sharp bend prior to the descent into the Manifold Valley. It has since been removed. The view is to Beeston Tor

Waterfall

Also removed are all of our wooden roadsigns such as this one at Waterfall

Heading for home at the end of the day in the village's main street

The old post office

Two views taken some forty years ago. There has now been considerable development infilling the area between the core of the village and the church, off left. Below: the view from the left of these cottages back to this junction. We no longer see milkchurns, which were finally phased out on 1st August 1979, when the last local delivery was made to Nestlés at Ashbourne

Two views of the former tollbar. It has now been extended, rendered and painted and the porch has been removed

(This page and overleaf): The Leek arm of the Caldon Canal at Longsdon, prior to the restoration. These views were taken in the early 1960s

The canal in better days may be seen behind Wall Grange Station. The latter opened in 1876. This photograph was taken on the last day of regular passenger service between Leek and The Potteries, 5th May, 1956. In the distance may be seen the water tower of Cheddleton Hospital

Sheffield House (on the right and behind the cart). The building was once a public house, owned by the Sheffield Brewery, hence its name. Note the sack cart at the top of the steps and the beer barrel on the pavement

Another view of Sheffield House and a wagon loaded with passengers. There is a small trap and horse behind the wagon waiting patiently. Beyond, the shop front is being repainted

Two views of the Cheshire Cheese Inn. The landlord was Thirza Robinson when the above photograph was taken. The building above right which blocked the road has now been removed

The Market Place at Longnor.

Driving sheep at Town Head

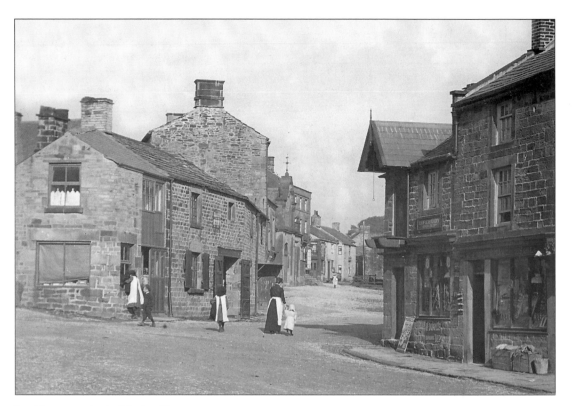

Looking towards the Market Place

In about 1970, Severn Trent proposed to build a new reservoir either above Winkhill, flooding Ford, or at Brund on the River Manifold. Eventually the plans were abandoned in favour of Carsington Water. This photograph indicates how shallow the Manifold reservoir would have been; even John Betjeman opposed it. This was the second proposal to inundate the Manifold. A previous scheme twenty or so years before being defeated in the House of Lords

Meerbrook and Tittesworth

Two photographs of the original Tittesworth or "New Pool" dam and the cottage which existed at its base until the new dam was built. The mock half-timbered appearance was how the house was constructed. Its seemed to lose its dignity when it was removed

Construction of the new road and bridge at Meerbrook as part of the reservoir redevelopment. There were two or three houses which were demolished alongside the road to Leek, behind the telegraph pole

Oakamoor

Filling a water barrel in Oakamoor close to The Cricketer's pub. The view is towards The Square

The old lime kiln in the village at the bottom of Star Bank, opposite the site of the toll house. It is now mostly hidden by trees and the petrol pumps of the Dell Filling Station have been removed

This celebration is unknown but of particular interest is the toll house on the Blythe Marsh (near Meir) to Thorpe turnpike. It was on the corner of the road to Whiston. Beyond it are The Cricketers Inn (left) and The Square (right)

Looking towards Jimmy's Yard and The Lord Nelson Inn, Oakamoor. The area is now developed with housing but the cottage and former blacksmiths beyond survive as dwellings

A Primitive Methodist meeting at Jimmy's Yard. The speaker is standing in the goods wagon seen on the far left

A quiet day in Mill Lane. The lady is walking towards the Coffee House Tavern. It was opened by the daughters of AS Bolton, the owner of the adjacent works. All the buildings shown here except the Coffee House, now called The Admiral Jervis, have been demolished. It used to have a billiard room upstairs. The lady is outside the old post office

Taken prior to 1923, these houses were built beyond Jimmys Yard

Okeover

An unusual sight these days – free range hens scratching across a field by the River Dove at Okeover. This was actually taken on the Derbyshire bank of the river

Sheen

Outlow Villa at Sheen

Rudyard and the Lake

As a result of a disagreement, the house to the left had its view of the Lake blocked by the construction of the house on the right – hence its name Spite Hall!

The Water Bailiff's Cottage built in 1852 to replace his previous house which became the Rudyard Lake Hotel

The Boer War memorial in Rudyard village. It was built to commemorate the Queen's Diamond Jubilee of 1897

Rudyard Lake in 1868. The railway cutting of 1849 had still to blend into the landscape. This must have been a dry summer for the water level is rather low

A Trades Union gathering on 22nd June, 1907, in the field by Spite Hall

Mrs. HEATH,
Spite Hall, Rudyard Vale.

Large or small parties catered for.   Apartments.
The finest Tea Gardens and Pavilion in Rudyard.
:: :: Motor and Rowing Boats for Hire. :: ::

TERMS VERY MODERATE.

Mrs Heath was one of several establishments catering for visitors

Several chalets were built around the Lake and this was the first purpose built cafe to be opened in 1906. It was run by the Guillard family of Leek

A striking view of what is believed to be the fish farm built by the monks of Dieulacresse Abbey at Pool End (hence the name). The dam must have held back quite a lot of water. The view was taken 40 years ago

Stanley

The floods in Stanley, in July 1927 after a severe thunderstorm raged over Leek and surrounding areas. Significant damage occurred in Stanley, Endon and Stockton Brook when a pool below Stanley Pool burst its banks

The first house here is Brook Cottage. At the beginning of the 20th Century, when this photograph was taken, it offered refreshments to hikers. The cottage was part of the Swythamley estate and was occupied by Frederick Brookes, a dyer at Tatton's mill nearby. Once a month he had to walk to Swythamley Hall to pay the rent (6d a week).– see *Images of Edwardian Leek* p76

The same cottages forty years ago. Excessive flooding occurred here a few years ago when the adjacent stream overflowed its banks

You could be forgiven for thinking that this view of Hen Cloud hasn't changed much. The mid-distance is now dominated by a huge range of agricultural buildings. Also, Tatton's chimney at the dyehouse has now been removed

When the Duchess of Teck visited the Roaches in 1872, this seat was cut so that she could admire the view in comfort

The Winking Eye Rock before he lost half of his nose! He looks down onto the Leek – Buxton road at Ramshaw Rocks. For the benefit of non-locals, he winks as you pass him. One cannot help but think that his features were aided by an adventurous stonemason

Warslow

A tranquil scene in the village opposite the shop

Taking a break outside the gates to Warslow Hall

Laying the foundation stones of the Village Hall. It opened in 1935

Waterhouses

The main road through the village in Edwardian times. The building on the left is now a house. At the other end of this terrace is the current village shop with The Crown Inn beyond it

The former NSR Goods Shed at Waterhouses in 1975. It is amazing that it survived at all. It is now part of the cycle hire centre. It was brought here from Fenton Station by the North Staffordshire Railway in 1905 at a cost of £175

The former railway bridge – it still survives – on the Waterhouses to Leek line, spanning the road to Cauldon Low. It was built in 1903 and was perhaps the last large one to be built in North Staffordshire, excluding major road scemes such as the M6

Thors Cave from the Wetton road. The photograph is undated but was probably taken about 100 years ago by WH Nithsdale

Thors Cave in 1894. The river bed was soon to be diverted to allow room for the Light Railway track

Ossums Crag near Wetton Mill during the excavation of the Eyrie Cave near the top of the face in 1956. The cave is twenty feet below the cliff top. Charcoal was found at a depth of eighteen inches indicating that it had been occupied by more than birds at

some point. The excavation was controlled by radio link and the rope used for lowering soil and finds may be seen hanging down the cliff face. Fortunately, the team leader, Don Bramwell, was an expert on bird bones!

The village pond at Wetton in the early 1960s. It was later filled in and converted to a carpark

Wetton Mill Bridge, built by the Duke of Devonshire at a cost of £184, after the previous structure was lost in a flood in 1807. The mill pond was in the foreground. The mill dates from 1711 when the former mill was replaced by the Duke with a new mill and kiln house. See *The Copper & Lead Mines around the Manifold Valley* for more historical detail on this and West Side Mill, near Ecton

The ford at Wetton Mill before the river bed was lined with concrete, creating an ugly scar we are stuck with

Index

Subscribers List

Mrs DC Ball, Blackshaw Moor
Mrs E Barks, Leek
Mrs JM Bennett, Leek
Mrs Biddulph, Leek
Michael Birch, Leek
Mr Birchall, Leek
Mr GJ Bloore, Leek
Bookthrift, Ashbourne
Bookthrift, Macclesfield
Colin Bowyer, Leek
Kenneth Bowyer, Leek
Mrs DE Brentnall, Leek
Janet Broome, Leek
Brian Brookes, Leek
DB Brookes, Leek
John Brough, Leek
John R Burgess, Leek
Roger S Burgess, Leek
Janet Burrows, Leek
Mr S Callear, Leek
Chapter One, Leek
Ray & Caroline Cork, Ashbourne
Derby City Library
Mrs M Deaville, Lichfield
Tim Eades, Alstonefield
Valerie Emery, Leek
Ralph Fleming, Leek
Raymond Fletcher, Leek

David & Beverley Foster, Leek
Bob Gratton, Dronfield
Pamela Hurst, Leek
Marian Hulme, Leek
Mrs Joan Jones, Leek
Mrs A Keates, Leek
John Newall, Leek
Mr JA Pickford, Endon
Picture Book, Leek
Potteries Museum, Hanley
David Rhead, Leek
Judith C Rider, Leek
J Robinson, Endon
Tony Smith, Leek
Severn Trent Water, Tittesworth Reservoir Visitor Centre
Ron Scholes, Leek
Staffordshire Moorlands Tourist Information Centre
Mr FR Stubbs, Endon
Jim Stubbs, Leek
Basil Turner, Leek
Kathleen Turner, Leek
Jonathan and Trudi Walton Leek
Wendy Walton, Leek
Janet & Roger Warrillow, Leek
John White, Leek
Kathleen Williamson, Leek